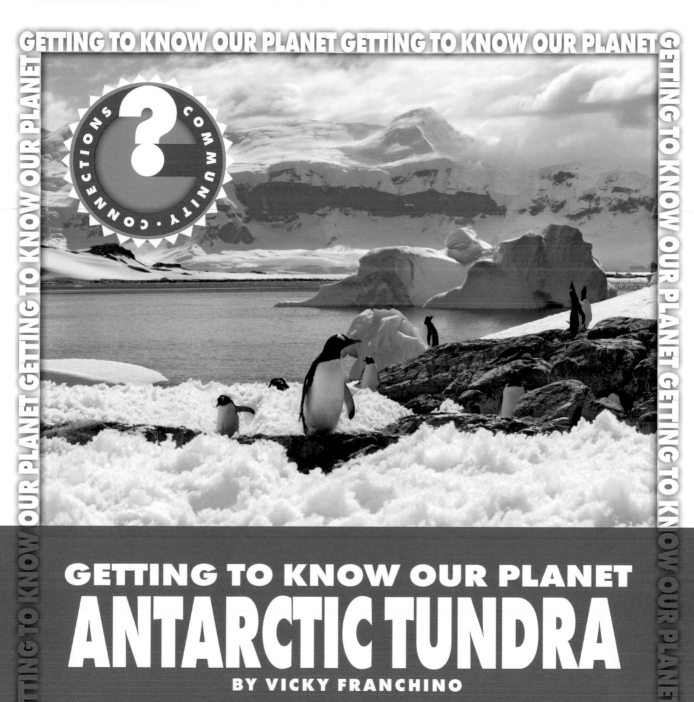

GETTING TO KNOW OUR PLANET GETTING TO KNOW OUR PLANET
GETTING TO KNOW OUR PLANET GETTING TO KNOW OUR PLANET
GETTING TO KNOW OUR PLANET GETTING TO KNOW OUR PLANET

COMMUNITY · CONNECTIONS

GETTING TO KNOW OUR PLANET
ANTARCTIC TUNDRA

BY VICKY FRANCHINO

Published in the United States of America by Cherry Lake Publishing
Ann Arbor, Michigan
www.cherrylakepublishing.com

Content Adviser: Linda M. Hooper-Bùi, PhD, Associate Professor, Department of Environmental Science, Louisiana State University Agricultural Center, Baton Rouge, Louisiana
Reading Adviser: Marla Conn, Read With Me Now

Photo Credits: Cover and page 1, © iStockphoto.com/Photodynamic; page 5, © Bernhard Staehli/Shutterstock.com; page 7, © Volodymyr Goinyk/Shutterstock.com; page 9, © Armin Rose/Shutterstock.com; pages 11, 13, 15, and 17, © Dmytro Pylypenko/Shutterstock.com; page 19, © Footage.Pro/Shutterstock.com; page 21, © erwinf./Shutterstock.com.

LIBRARY OF CONGRESS CATALOGING-IN-PUBLICATION DATA

Franchino, Vicky.
  Antarctic tundra / by Vicky Franchino.
      pages cm. — (Community connections) (Getting to know our planet)
  Includes bibliographical references and index.
  ISBN 978-1-63470-514-1 (lib. bdg.) — ISBN 978-1-63470-574-5 (pdf) — ISBN 978-1-63470-634-6 (pbk.) — ISBN 978-1-63470-694-0 (ebook)
  1. Tundra ecology—Arctic regions—Juvenile literature. 2. Tundras—Arctic regions—Juvenile literature. I. Title.
  QH541.5.T8.F735 2015
  577.5'86—dc23   2015028523

Cherry Lake Publishing would like to acknowledge the work of The Partnership for 21st Century Skills.
Please visit www.p21.org for more information.

Printed in the United States of America
Corporate Graphics
January 2016

ANTARCTIC TUNDRA

CONTENTS

THE COLDEST PLACE ON EARTH

The ground is always frozen in the Antarctic **tundra**. The temperature there falls to −75 degrees Fahrenheit (−59 degrees Celsius) in the winter. In summer, it is just above freezing. The snow and ice there never melt. Over time, layers of snow press on each other. They become hard as rock, forming a **glacier**.

Pieces of glaciers sometimes break off and fall into the ocean.

What do you already know about Antarctica? What would you like to learn about this place? Write down your questions. See if you can find the answers in this book!

Antarctica is the fifth-largest **continent**. It is found at the southern end of Earth. The seasons in Antarctica are the opposite of those in the United States. It is winter from March to September. It is summer from October to February. In the winter, it is dark nearly all the time. In the summer, there are days when the sun never sets.

6

The sun can be very bright in Antarctica.

THINK!

Can you imagine living in a place where it is light or dark all the time? What would you do for fun in the dark? Would you be able to sleep if the sun was shining all night?

7

A WORLD OF WHITE

Antarctica is covered with a thick layer of ice. In some places, the ice is more than 1 mile (1.6 kilometers) thick! Hidden beneath this frozen covering are mountains, valleys, and even volcanoes. In some places, there are deep cracks in the ice called **crevasses**. Don't fall in! A crevasse can be 100 feet (30.5 meters) deep.

Crevasses can form as glaciers begin to break apart.

What if you woke up one morning to find your hometown covered in a thick layer of ice like Antarctica? Write a short story describing what would happen. How would you get to school? How would you stay warm?

Not many things can live in a place that is so cold and dark. There are no trees or bushes in Antarctica. The only plants that can survive are liverwort, moss, lichen, and algae. These plants are very short. This means the wind can't blow them over.

Mosses are some of the only plants that can survive Antarctica's harsh weather.

LOOK!

Look at the plants in your backyard or a nearby park. Do any of them look like the plants in Antarctica? How are they the same? How are they different?

11

ANIMALS IN A FROZEN LAND

Very few animals live in Antarctica's harsh **climate**. Those that do have special features to protect them. Penguins, whales, and seals have **blubber**. This is a thick layer of fat that **insulates** them from the cold. Penguins also have feathers that are covered with a special oil to block wind and water. Seals have a warm fur coat.

Seals can stay warm even while swimming in icy water.

THINK!

For animals in the Antarctic tundra, staying dry is just as important as staying warm. Why do you think this is? Think about what happens when you go outside with wet hair on a cold day.

13

A number of birds can be found in Antarctica. The wandering albatross only comes onshore to lay eggs and care for its chicks. Its wingspan is 12 feet (3.6 m) wide. This is the widest wingspan of any bird. The Antarctic petrel dives into the icy water to find food. And look for the South Polar skua. This bird eats baby penguins as well as the eggs of other birds.

Antarctic petrels eat fish and other small sea creatures.

Scientists have discovered that Earth's climate is getting warmer. How could warmer temperatures change Antarctica? How could this affect the animals and plants that live there? Look for books and articles to read about what scientists are predicting.

15

The cold waters surrounding Antarctica are home to many sea creatures. The scaleless icefish has special blood that doesn't freeze. Orcas are the largest member of the dolphin family. They can weigh up to 10 tons. Krill are only 2 inches (5 centimeters) long. However, they are the favorite food of whales and many other large sea animals.

Huge amounts of krill live in the waters surrounding Antarctica.

You don't have to worry about bug bites if you visit Antarctica. The only insect on the continent is the midge. A midge is a type of fly. Look at the insects that live near your house. Then compare them with the midge. Do you think they could survive in Antarctica? Why or why not?

WHO LIVES IN ANTARCTICA?

You might not be surprised to learn that few people live in Antarctica. It is too cold to grow food there. There is little fresh water. Most of the year, people can't survive outside for very long. The only people who go to Antarctica are scientists and explorers. They travel there on helicopters, airplanes, or special boats that can break through ice.

Traveling to Antarctica can be very difficult.

THINK!

How would you get food and drinking water if you lived in Antarctica? How would you stay warm? How would you travel from one place to another? What if you needed a doctor? None of these things are easy to find in Antarctica.

Scientists in Antarctica live and work at research stations. They learn about things such as **geology**, weather, and climate change. Most stations are near the coast. This makes it easier to deliver supplies to them.

Would you like to visit Antarctica? Perhaps you will be a scientist one day. You can help study this amazing continent!

Antarctica's researchers are incredibly far from any towns or cities.

Try drawing a picture based on what you know about Antarctica. You could draw one of the animals that live there. Or you could imagine what the world might look like under the thick layer of ice that covers the continent. Be creative!

21

GLOSSARY

blubber (BLUHB-ur) the layer of fat under the skin of a whale, seal, or other large marine animal

climate (KLYE-mit) the weather typical of a place over a long period of time

continent (KAHN-tuh-nuhnt) one of the seven large landmasses of Earth

crevasses (KREV-uhs-iz) deep, open cracks, especially in a glacier

geology (jee-AH-luh-jee) the study of Earth's layers of soil and rock

glacier (GLAY-shur) a slow-moving mass of ice found in mountain valleys or polar regions

insulates (IN-suh-layts) prevents heat from escaping

tundra (TUHN-druh) a very cold area where there are no trees and the soil under the surface is always frozen

FIND OUT MORE

BOOKS

Britton, Arthur K. *Life at a Polar Research Station*. New York: Gareth Stevens, 2013.

Spilsbury, Louise, and Richard Spilsbury. *Southern Ocean*. Chicago: Capstone Heinemann Library, 2015.

Taylor, Barbara. *Arctic & Antarctic*. New York: DK Publishing, 2012.

WEB SITES

National Geographic Kids—Crittercam: Antarctic Adventure
http://kids.nationalgeographic.com/kids/games /geographygames/crittercamantarctic
Can you rescue the critter cams and recover the movies they hold? This game is a fun way to learn about Antarctica.

TIME for Kids—Antarctica
www.timeforkids.com/minisite/antarctica
Learn amazing fun facts about life in Antarctica!

INDEX

ABOUT THE AUTHOR

Vicky Franchino loves to discover new places, animals, and plants and has written many books about the natural world. Although it was fun to learn about Antarctica, Vicky does not particularly want to visit it because she does not like cold weather. She *has* seen a glacier in Canada, which was quite exciting! Vicky lives in Wisconsin with her family, where there is a lot of cold weather but not as much as there is in Antarctica.